MW01132896

Marjorie Kinnan Rawlings and the Florida Crackers

Ms. Rawlings writing outdoors. *(Courtesy of the State Archives of Florida)*

Marjorie Kinnan Rawlings and the Florida Crackers

Sandra Wallus Sammons

Pineapple Press, Inc.
Sarasota, Florida

To my mother, Elsie L. Wallus, who always wanted to write, and to Sharon Waters, artist, poet, and friend.

Manufactured April 2010

Inquiries should be addressed to:

Pineapple Press, Inc.
P.O. Box 3889
Sarasota, Florida 34230

www.pineapplepress.com

Library of Congress Cataloging-in-Publication Data

Sammons, Sandra Wallus.
Marjorie Kinnan Rawlings and the Florida Crackers / by Sandra Wallus Sammons. -- 1st ed.
p. cm.
Includes bibliographical references and index.
ISBN 978-1-56164-472-8 (alk. paper) -- ISBN 978-1-56164-473-5 (pbk. : alk. paper)
1. Rawlings, Marjorie Kinnan, 1896-1953--Homes and haunts--Florida--Juvenile literature. 2. Authors, American--20th century--Biography--Juvenile literature. 3. Authors, American--Homes and haunts--Florida--Juvenile literature 4. Frontier and pioneer life--Florida--Juvenile literature. 5. Florida--Intellectual life--Juvenile literature. I. Title. II. Title: Marjorie Kinnan Rawlings.
PS3535.A845Z844 2010
813'.52--dc20
[B]

2010006666

First Edition

Design by Shé Hicks

Contents

Foreword

Marjorie Kinnan Rawlings loved to tell stories, even when she was a young child. When she learned how to write, she wrote stories on anything that was handy. If she couldn't find a sheet of paper, she would write on paper bags! Her parents were delighted by her interest. They told her that she didn't have to do jobs around the house when she was busy writing.

Later, Marjorie wanted very much to have her stories published. However, she did not have much success until she and her husband moved to Florida. There she met people who had contentedly lived in the deep woods for years. These people were called "Crackers." Their way of life fascinated her, so she began writing stories about them. Marjorie wrote with such excitement and enthusiasm that her stories finally were published.

She became one of Florida's best-known authors. Her books were read around the world. She won many prizes for her writing, including the Pulitzer Prize for fiction in 1939. But for Marjorie Kinnan Rawlings, awards were just a bonus. Most important to her was that she had realized her dream of becoming a writer. She wrote and told exciting stories that people still read today. Her work tells us of days long ago in Florida's fascinating history.

“Look deep into nature, and then you will understand everything better.”

—Albert Einstein

Chapter 1

The Young Writer

Marjorie Kinnan was born a city girl. Her parents, Arthur and Ida Kinnan, were living in the capital of the United States, Washington, D.C., when she was born. They welcomed her into the world on August 8, 1896. Her father loved spending time in the country too, though. He often took his daughter to a farm he owned in nearby Maryland. There, Arthur Kinnan and the girl he called "Peaches" and "the joy of my life" spent many happy hours together. They would go walking outdoors in both rain and sunshine. Arthur Kinnan inspired his daughter to love nature. Even years later, Marjorie remembered those walks fondly.

Young Marjorie also visited her grandparents' farm in Michigan. That's where she learned the sheer joy of picking and eating the very fresh foods out of their bountiful garden. Her grandmother's cookies,

Marjorie Kinnan as a baby.
(From Marjorie Kinnan Rawlings Collection, Department of Special and Area Studies Collections, George A. Smathers Libraries, University of Florida)

fresh from the oven, were also tempting. Later, when Marjorie had her own kitchen, she loved cooking. She even wrote a cookbook.

Both her parents encouraged her to tell, read, and write stories. They wanted her to use her imagination. Marjorie told stories to any neighborhood children who would listen while she was growing up. When she was eleven years old, one of her little stories was printed in *The Washington Post*, a popular newspaper. She won a two-dollar prize. More importantly, she learned that people appreciated the words she wrote.

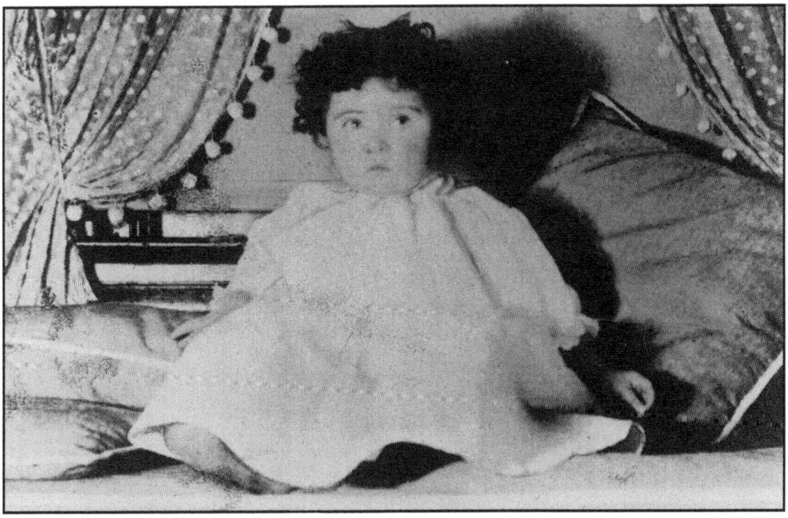

Marjorie at the age of four. (From Marjorie Kinnan Rawlings Collection, Department of Special and Area Studies Collections, George A. Smathers Libraries, University of Florida)

Marjorie continued to write when she was in high school. When she was seventeen, her father died. She missed him very much. However, she knew that his love and respect of nature would stay with her for the rest of her life.

Marjorie moved to Madison, Wisconsin, with her mother and her brother. Arthur. There she became an English major at the University of Wisconsin. She continued to write stories, plays, and poems. Some of her writing was published in the college literary magazine. Marjorie did well in all her courses and graduated with honors.

Then came the big decision. Where should she live to start a career as a writer? New York was a fast-growing city in the early 1900s. It was also known as a place where many writers got recognized for their talent. She had always lived in cities, so perhaps it was the place for her. She decided to take the chance.

Marjorie's suitcase held just a few clothes, and a lot of her best poems and stories. Surely she would be able to sell her writing in New York. That would have to happen soon, though. She had only sixty dollars in her pocket!

While Marjorie was out looking for work, the unexpected happened. A thief stole all her money. Later Marjorie had to laugh, though, because even the thief didn't bother to take her little packet of stories. She had not found a publisher who would print them. Maybe they weren't even worth stealing!

A friend loaned her twenty dollars so she could pay for food and a place to live until she got a job. She started work at the YWCA, the Young Women's Christian Association. Her job was to edit other people's writing. Although she was happy to have a job, she really wanted to be writing her own stories. She also started writing letters to Charles Rawlings. She had met him at the University of Wisconsin when they both worked on the college magazine. He wanted to become a writer too. When Charles came to New York, they realized they wanted to be together all the time. Marjorie Kinnan and Charles Rawlings were married in May of 1919.

The couple moved to Louisville, Kentucky, and then to Charles' home city of Rochester, New York. They found jobs in sales and writing articles for newspapers. For two years, Marjorie wrote a popular article called "Songs of the Housewife." She described the joys of raising children and keeping the house

Charles and Marjorie Rawlings. *(Courtesy of the State Archives of Florida)*

clean, even though she didn't have any children and didn't like housework. She proved she had a good imagination! When she had time, Marjorie continued to write her own stories.

Marjorie spent almost ten years working for others and trying to get her stories published. But she still hadn't gotten her big break. Marjorie was disappointed. She and Charles were also having marriage problems.

It was winter. The young couple decided to leave the cold New York weather for a vacation in warm Florida. They visited Charles' brothers, Wray and James, who owned land in the north-central part of the state. When the boat carrying the Rawlingses docked in Jacksonville, they were met by Zelma Cason. She was one of the brothers' friends. Together they traveled along a bumpy road to Island Grove, a small town just a few miles from Cross Creek.

Marjorie loved Florida! When she saw the beauty of the land and met some of the people there, the young author suddenly felt a new energy. She turned to Charles and exclaimed: "Let's sell everything and move South! How we could write!" The decision was made.

Chapter 2

The Crackers

Charles asked his brothers to look for a house and land for them in the country near Island Grove. Although they had no experience with farming in Florida, Marjorie and Charles wanted to buy an already planted orange grove. They hoped that the sale of oranges might give them enough money to live on until their published writings could provide a regular income. They hoped too that this total change from city to country life would be good for their marriage.

In the summer of 1928, the Rawlings bought an old house and about seventy acres of land without even seeing them first! Their new home would be in an area known as Cross Creek. The name came from the nearby small creek, just a mile long, that "crossed" between Lake Lochloosa and Orange Lake.

They eagerly moved south in November. When

they arrived, they looked over their new property, with its grove of about 3,000 citrus trees. They hoped for a large harvest of oranges, grapefruit, and tangerines the following winter. It would be a huge amount of work, but they were determined. Looking further, they also found that they had pecan trees, chickens, two mules, a tenant house, an eight-room farmhouse, and a barn. Later, Marjorie added dogs, cats, ducks, and a raccoon named "Racket." Marjorie Kinnan Rawlings, even though she had born in a northern city, had a feeling that she had finally found "home."

There was so much work to be done. In the beginning, Wray and James came to the grove to help as often as they could. The farm was even named *Los Hermanos*, which is Spanish for "The Brothers."

But there was an even bigger challenge. Marjorie and Charles were city folk living deep in the Florida woods. There were no stores nearby. They were about four miles from Island Grove and about twenty-five miles from the larger town of Gainesville. Could they possibly live in the Florida backwoods like the other people living near Cross Creek? The "Crackers," as they were called, seemed to get along very well without going out and buying what they needed.

Marjorie looked closely at her neighbors. They

The Rawlings' home at Cross Creek (From Marjorie Kinnan Rawlings Collection, Department of Special and Area Studies Collections, George A. Smathers Libraries, University of Florida)

didn't own much, but they seemed perfectly happy in their own world. "Cracker" was the name given to some of the early settlers in the backwoods. No one knows for sure how they got that name. Perhaps it was because of their lifestyle. They *cracked* their whips as they moved cattle from place to place. They *cracked*, or crushed, corn to make grits and cornmeal.

Whatever the reason, the Florida Cracker way of life fascinated Marjorie. Almost immediately, Marjorie started making notes about the way they lived. Her neighbors were so different from any people she had known before!

The Crackers lived simply. Although others might

think of them as poor, they were contented with their lives in the backwoods. Instead of buying a broom, they took leaves from a palm tree or palmetto and made one to keep their small, tin-roofed houses clean. Palm leaves were also used to make hats for their heads, to shield them from the hot Florida sun. They planted gardens, and they hunted and fished for their food. Water for drinking was carried from a nearby well. Even though people living in large cities had washing machines, the women at Cross Creek still heated water in an iron kettle and hand-washed their clothes. They "made do" with whatever was nearby and lived in harmony with the land around them.

The Crackers that Marjorie met had also learned to be at peace with the wild nature of the place. The woods were filled with birds, flowers, sunshine, and beauty. They were also filled with wild animals such as bears, alligators, and snakes. Light rains that came in the spring were soft and good for the gardens. Heavy thunderstorms that came during the summer brought lightning and floods. The Crackers accepted the good with the bad, simply because they had chosen the woods to be their home.

Some of Marjorie's neighbors, the Will Mickens family, outside her home at Cross Creek. (*Courtesy of the State Archives of Florida*)

Chapter 3

A New Excitement

When Charles and Marjorie first moved to Cross Creek, there wasn't much time for thinking or writing. The jobs were never-ending. Living at *Los Hermanos* kept them busy, since each day they had to tend the groves, garden, and animals.

They struggled for over a year. Charles wrote articles that he sold so they could pay some bills. Marjorie squeezed in time to jot down some quick notes about the fascinating things around her. Charles enjoyed traveling away from the hard work at Cross Creek, but Marjorie was slowly but surely feeling more at home.

Maybe she was remembering the walks through country woods with her father. Maybe she simply had a natural love for the country life. Either way, Marjorie Kinnan Rawlings, the city girl, became totally absorbed in studying the people, weather, and wildlife around her. Living at Cross Creek was like the dawning of a new day, with the sun coming over the horizon and making everything clear. She began to understand

Cross Creek. *(Courtesy of the State Archives of Florida)*

why these country people were content. There *was* something truly special about these deep Florida backwoods.

Instead of thinking of the orange grove as a huge job, she became fascinated with the trees and their fruit. She noticed the delicious smell of the blossoms, and she then watched with her eyes wide open as the pea-sized fruit grew bigger, turning from dark green into bright orange, ripe fruit. Her imagination went off in all directions. She even thought that the oranges looked like golden lanterns on the trees. Rather than picking them early for the best price at market, she put off picking them as long as she could!

Whenever she could take the time, Marjorie went for long walks in the woods. At first, the plants had been strange to her. But soon she recognized the differences between gallberry and sparkleberry, ti-ti and spiderwort. She noticed that Spanish moss, so abundant on the trees, had tiny rose-colored flowers in the early spring. They were almost invisible to those who did not look carefully, but she did. She found patches of ripe wild strawberries, and Marjorie ate her fill with a smile on her face.

Nothing escaped her notice. Tiny insects and small green rain frogs suddenly were fascinating. She soon

knew which birds were nearby just by their songs or by the way they flapped their wings. She noticed the rhythm of Florida's seasons. Weather in the South might seem like summer all the time, but Marjorie knew that there were many changes during the year. You just had to look for them. If you were aware of nature around you, seasons were obvious. She realized that if you just got to know when certain birds built their nests or when certain types of flowers bloomed, then you would never need a calendar.

Marjorie was terrified of snakes when she first arrived at Cross Creek. But Marjorie had chosen Cross Creek for her home, and snakes had lived there for years before she arrived. She finally got used to seeing them in her yard and in the woods. She was not pleased, however, when they got into her house. One day she reached for a plate in her kitchen cabinet and came face to face with a big snake!

She was always watchful of the reptiles, but became less afraid and more curious. There was a snake crossing near her house. Snakes took that path just as we would take a road. She even began to watch for a friendly black snake that would crawl up the post by her gate. She was definitely settling in to feeling at home in the deep Florida woods.

Marjorie Kinnan Rawlings by her garden gate. Is she watching for her pet snake? (*Courtesy of the State Archives of Florida*)

Marjorie Rawlings, the writer, realized that if she was so fascinated by the wildlife and the weather and the people living there, she should do something about it. She decided to write about them and get those stories published.

After each walk, she spent hours writing in her notebooks, describing a snake or a bird or a person in great detail. She wrote as fast as she could, while the thoughts were fresh in her mind. Soon the notes were turned into stories. She knew that Cross Creek and the Florida Crackers' way of life was a fresh new subject for her. It was also one that brought her great excitement.

She also realized that the Cross Creek way of life would change, since many other people were moving to that area. The deep woods were being sold so that new houses could be built. Marjorie and the Florida Crackers lived in small, older homes that some of the first settlers there had built and used. With modern times coming to Cross Creek, the old Cracker way of life would change, and it would probably never be the same again. She decided she wanted to write, and write quickly, about the magical place she had found. She wanted to tell her readers all about it.

Chapter 4

The Right Subject

Charles made a table for Marjorie from the trunk of a palm tree. Marjorie put her typewriter on top, pulled up a chair, sat down, and wrote for hours. If her neighbors walked by while she was deep in thought about a story, they would respect her need for quiet time. They would walk on by without even calling out "Hello."

It was important to Marjorie that every word be exactly right. She would type, and then sometimes pull the paper out of the typewriter if she didn't like it. She'd crumple the page up and throw it on the floor. Then she would start typing again. Although she loved writing and believed in her stories, it was definitely hard work to actually get just exactly the right words on the blank sheet of paper.

Marjorie met the neighbors who lived near her home at Cross Creek, as well as in the Florida back-

Ms. Rawlings writing outdoors. *(Courtesy of the State Archives of Florida)*

woods around them, called the Big Scrub. She overflowed with ideas, wanting to quickly describe in words what she learned about these fascinating people every day. She wrote and wrote, and crumpled up one page after another. Finally, she thought she was ready to send some of her stories to a New York publisher. She told her friends that if *those* stories were not published, she would stop writing.

Marjorie waited. And waited. Finally, she heard that the very first stories she had sent out had been accepted for publication by *Scribner's Magazine*.

A dirt road through the palmettos and pine trees of the Big Scrub.
(Courtesy of the State Archives of Florida)

Cracker Chidlings: Real Tales from the Florida Interior was the title of her short story collection. In March 1930, she received a check for $150 and sighed with relief. It was not a large amount of money, but it meant a lot to her. After all, this was a major event in her life. She was thirty-three years old, and had been writing for years. In writing about the people and the countryside around her, she had finally become a published Florida author. Marjorie had found her subject, one that fascinated her. Easier times were about to start!

Every day Marjorie learned more about her neighbors and the way they lived. And every day her respect for them grew. Her neighbors learned more about Marjorie too. Soon she was no longer seen as an outsider. Rather, she was accepted as a trusted friend in their community. They could see that this newcomer appreciated their way of life.

Marjorie and Charles had no children of their own. Neighborhood children loved to visit with "Miz Rawlins." The children would crawl under her house to find eggs that the hens had laid. They would follow Mother Duck and her ducklings as they honked their way to the tub of water in the backyard. Marjorie would also give the children cornbread. They crumbled it into glasses filled with fresh milk from Dora the cow. What a treat!

Marjorie had friends and a rich, full life at the Creek. She was a vivacious woman, full of life and energy. She felt that she had chosen well in making this place her home, and she lived every minute to its fullest.

Her writing, however, was serious business. She wanted to record, accurately, what was happening around her. She wanted the characters in her stories to be as close as possible to the real people she had gotten to know. Sometimes when people live in small groups, away from other people, they make up much of their own way of talking. This is known as dialect. Marjorie faithfully copied that dialect for her stories. For example, instead of saying "ants," the Crackers would say "antses." The red-bird, or cardinal, was called the "reddy-bird."

Marjorie's Cracker neighbors were amazed at how the characters in her stories spoke the same way they did. But Marjorie had concentrated on not only what was said. She had also paid attention to *how* her neighbors spoke. She had listened to every word carefully. Then she had written their dialect down on paper. Therefore, she had gotten the words in her books exactly right.

And Marjorie herself had changed. In some ways, she was living more like her Cracker neighbors. The girl from the city went on deer hunts. She went out on a boat to catch her own crabs for dinner. She went to square dances. She was learning the ways of the Crackers, and she was having fun!

Chapter 5

The Words Start Flowing

After *Cracker Chidlings* was published, Marjorie was inspired to write even more stories. Every day she had more ideas of stories about the Crackers. More and more balls of paper fell to the floor next to her typewriter on the palm-tree table.

Next to be published was "Jacob's Ladder." She received a check for $700 for the story in December of 1930. She thought she had received a fortune. Marjorie paid some of her bills. She also had a bathroom put inside her house. She was tired of going out back to the outhouse! When the indoor bathroom was completed, Marjorie had a party as a celebration. Her friends found ice and sodas for them in her brand-new bathtub.

Marjorie was so careful with each word in "Jacob's Ladder" that her readers could *feel* what she wanted to say. Each written word perfectly described the fury of a

An outhouse at the Marjorie Kinnan Rawlings Historic State Park today. *(Courtesy of the State Archives of Florida)*

hurricane that took place in the story. She had managed to paint a picture in words. Her readers could almost *see* the bending of the trees and the crashing of the floodwater through the Florida woods.

Maxwell Perkins, an editor at Scribner's in New York, read Marjorie's stories. He immediately knew this author had great talent. He became her editor. The two became great friends as Perkins continued to make suggestions about how to make her writing more successful. Letters between the two went back and forth. He wanted to read more about these very interesting Crackers. He also suggested that she write not just stories, but a novel.

Marjorie was thrilled at the suggestion, and ready for the challenge. She wrote back to Perkins, saying she was "vibrating with material like a hive of bees in swarm."

She went further in her research. She actually lived with the Fiddia family in their Big Scrub backwoods home for a while. She wanted to learn even more about how these fascinating people lived. Leonard Fiddia's mother, Piety, had white hair and weighed only ninety pounds, but she still plowed the fields behind a mule.

Leonard Fiddia (left) and a friend. (From Marjorie Kinnan Rawlings Collection, Department of Special and Area Studies Collections, George A. Smathers Libraries, University of Florida)

Leonard was a hunter, trapper, and fisherman. Marjorie took many, many notes on everything they told her.

Marjorie Kinnan Rawlings' first published novel was *South Moon Under*. It was, of course, about the Crackers in the central Florida woods. Again, Marjorie made sure every word was exactly right. Readers could almost hear the snap of branches as Marjorie described her characters walking through the woods. *South Moon Under* was a great success when it appeared in bookstores in 1933. An edition published in England was also very popular.

Although happy about finally being published, this was also a sad time for Marjorie. She and Charles had hoped their marriage would work. However, they had too many differences. After fourteen years together, they decided to divorce.

With Charles no longer helping to pay the bills, the money Marjorie made on her writing and selling oranges was just not enough. She liked to tell the story about the one day when the only food she had left to eat in her house was a box of crackers and a can of soup. On that very day, the mailman came with good news. She was awarded first prize for her short story "Gal Young 'Un" in the O. Henry Memorial Award contest. Inside the envelope was a check for $500!

Golden Apples was her next book. Marjorie used the words "golden apples" to describe ripe oranges, and the story was about an Englishman and Crackers living in Florida. Although she worked on the book for two years, she was never really happy with it. It was hard for her to write about an Englishman whom she had not known. It was much easier to write about the Crackers, whom she knew quite well by then. She realized that she should go back to writing totally about the Florida Crackers and their way of life.

While she was at work on *Golden Apples*, Cal Long, one of her neighbors, began sharing stories with her about when he was young. He told her about a pet deer his brother had when he was young, when their family lived in the deep woods of the Big Scrub. Cal told her many stories about their little fawn and how it got into trouble eating the fresh new vegetables out of their garden. Marjorie would remember that story when she started writing her next story. It was about a young Cracker boy, his parents, and his pet deer. That book would be called *The Yearling*.

Little did she know then that this story would be read and loved by people around the world.

Chapter 6

The Yearling

Again, Marjorie paid great attention to detail. She learned from her neighbors that Cracker children seldom spent much time in school. Instead the boys went fishing or hunting with their fathers to put meat on the table at suppertime. The boys also worked hard in the fields. Sometimes they were out there from sunup to sundown.

She learned about the animals in the woods. She even studied what a Florida deer looks like, in exact detail. She paid great attention to the typical Cracker homes and gardens, from the rough furniture to the vegetables they planted. She carefully examined the trees in the woods. She listened to the birds and the sounds of the pine trees swaying in the wind. She sniffed the smells of the fields and freshly-dug earth. To accurately describe the fear and excitement her

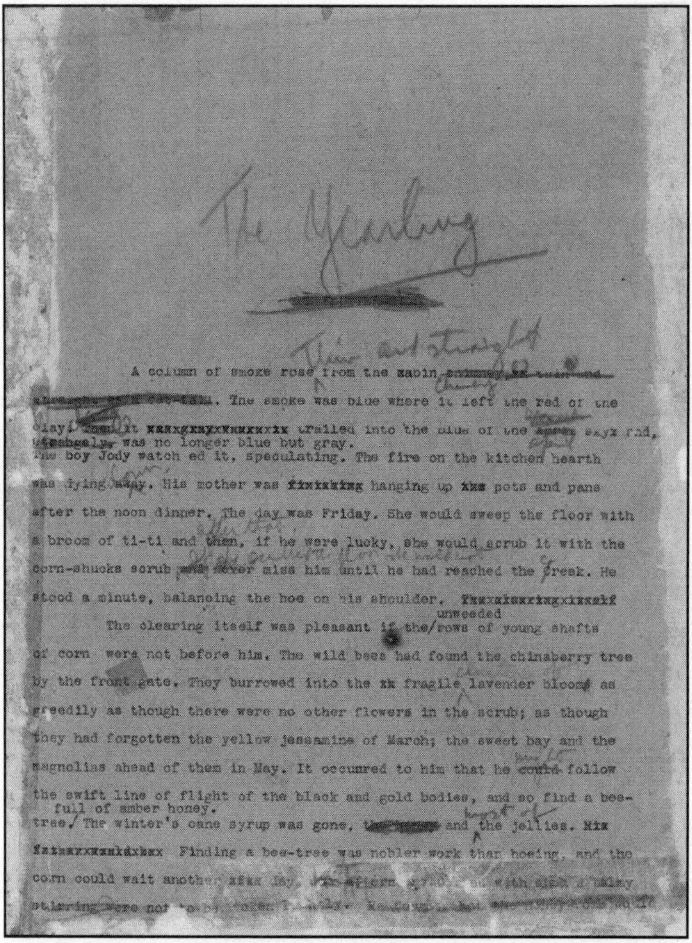

The Yearling

A column of smoke rose from the cabin . The smoke was blue where it left the red of the clay. it trailed into the blue of the sky and, was no longer blue but gray.
The boy Jody watch ed it, speculating. The fire on the kitchen hearth was dying . His mother was hanging up pots and pans after the noon dinner. The day was Friday. She would sweep the floor with a broom of ti-ti and , if he were lucky, she would scrub it with the corn-shucks scrub never miss him until he had reached the creek. He stood a minute, balancing the hoe on his shoulder.

The clearing itself was pleasant if the unweeded rows of young shafts of corn were not before him. The wild bees had found the chinaberry tree by the front gate. They burrowed into the fragile lavender blooms as greedily as though there were no other flowers in the scrub; as though they had forgotten the yellow jessamine of March; the sweet bay and the magnolias ahead of them in May. It occurred to him that he might follow the swift line of flight of the black and gold bodies, and so find a bee-tree full of amber honey. The winter's cane syrup was gone, and the jellies. Finding a bee-tree was nobler work than hoeing, and the corn could wait another day.

A page of The Yearling *that Marjorie wanted to get exactly right.* *(From Marjorie Kinnan Rawlings Collection, Department of Special and Area Studies Collections, George A. Smathers Libraries, University of Florida)* characters, Jody and his father, Penny Baxter, would feel on a bear hunt, Marjorie even went on a bear hunt herself!

Her story would be about a young boy growing up in the woods without brothers and sisters or games to play. Even alone, though, children found ways to have fun. Marjorie learned that boys would sometimes make a "flutter-mill." This was made from sticks and pieces of palm frond and placed next to a quickly-flowing stream. If you made it right, the palm frond would just catch the top of the water and spin, and was great fun to watch. She wrote down every little detail in her notes.

Finally, Marjorie felt she had enough notes. The trees, the animals, the people, and the place in her new story were almost real to her. She started to write. She went through many sheets of paper before she felt she had all the words right.

The result of all her hard work was *The Yearling*. It told the story of Jody Baxter, a twelve-year-old Cracker boy who lived with his mother and father deep in the Florida woods. One day Jody found a fawn, a baby deer, whose mother had been killed. He asked his Pa if he could take the fawn home because Jody wanted a pet that was all his own.

Part of the story describes how Jody came to

name his new pet. He visited Fodder-wing, another young boy who lived with his family a distance away. Fodder-wing had been sick during most of his life, but he had a great love for animals and had many pets. Unfortunately, when Jody arrived, he found that his friend had just died. Jody was very sad. He spent some time with Fodder-wing's family to join them in remembering his friend. While he was talking with Fodder-wing's mother, he learned that his friend had already named his deer. Fodder-wing knew that young deer have tails that wave almost like a flag, so he gave it the name "Flag."

A fawn like Flag. *(Courtesy of the State Archives of Florida)*

Jody was so happy that his good friend had named his new pet. He would have the company of something he could call his own, *and* his good friend had named it. The story described their hard life in the Florida woods. Marjorie Kinnan Rawlings clearly showed that she understood the ways of Cracker families.

When Marjorie sent a copy of *The Yearling* to her editor, Maxwell Perkins, he loved it. He wrote to Marjorie: "I'll tell you what *The Yearling* has done for me. You know how much there is to worry about when one goes to bed these nights. But my mind often goes to *The Yearling*—the country, people, and the hunts—and then all is good and happy. Now that's a test of how good a book is."

The book was published in 1938, just before the start of World War II. *The Yearling* won the Pulitzer Prize for fiction in 1939, one of the highest prizes in writing. It was translated into many different languages and sold around the world. The story would later also be made into a movie. All over the country and in many parts of the world, people enjoyed Marjorie Kinnan Rawlings' story about life in the Florida backwoods. She was not only writing about what she loved, but she was now famous too.

Chapter 7

The Famous Author

The next four years were good ones for Marjorie. Thousands of people wrote to tell her how much they enjoyed reading her book. One letter came from a naturalist, a person who had studied wild Florida for years. That reader thought Ms. Rawlings had described natural Florida very accurately. Another was from a twelve-year-old boy who wanted the author to know how much he had enjoyed reading the story about a boy his age and his pet fawn. She was asked to speak to groups in the United States and other parts of the world. Her readers wanted to hear more about Cross Creek and how she did her writing. Marjorie was happy to share what she had learned.

She was famous, and for the first time, she knew she could afford to stay at Cross Creek. The city girl now felt very comfortable in the Florida woods, with her many friends and neighbors around her. She also met other Florida authors, like Zora Neale Hurston, who lived in Eatonville, in the central part of the state. Ms. Hurston wrote stories about African-Americans, and Zora and Marjorie became close friends. She had a friendship with Marjory Stoneman Douglas, who lived near Miami in south Florida. Ms. Douglas was also fascinated with natural Florida and was known for speaking out to protect the Everglades. Marjory Stoneman Douglas wrote a letter to Marjorie Kinnan Rawlings saying that she thoroughly enjoyed reading *The Yearling*. Marjorie also met Robert Frost, the New England poet, and Margaret Mitchell of Atlanta, Georgia, the author of *Gone with the Wind.*

A very special treat was an invitation to the White House, in Washington, D.C. Marjorie was invited by Eleanor Roosevelt, the wife of Franklin Delano Roosevelt, America's thirty-second president.

Traveling and new friends did not change her feelings about the Florida woods. Cross Creek would always be "home" to Marjorie Kinnan Rawlings. She remodeled her old Cracker-style house for more comfort. And her dogs, Moe and Pat, and her cat, Smokey, were always glad to welcome her back.

Marjorie was a truly giving person and enjoyed

Marjorie sitting with her dog at Cross Creek. *(Courtesy of the State Archives of Florida)*

company and meeting new people. She was very generous and particularly liked to cook for her friends. Her meals were lovingly prepared and tasted wonderful. Dora the cow gave rich milk. Aunt Martha Mickens, Marjorie's helper, took cream from the milking bucket, put it into a churn, and made fresh butter. That butter, on just-baked, warm cornbread was delicious. Mmmmmm!

On a large dining table, meals were served on fine china, and guests used silver knives, forks, and spoons. The menu was certainly different, though. She served pot roast of bear or alligator-tail steak. Marjorie loved testing new recipes on her guests. Several months later, she completed a cookbook, *Cross Creek Cookery*. It included some of these unusual treats.

A very good friend, Norton Baskin, was often a guest at the dinner table. He was the manager of a hotel in St. Augustine, Florida. Marjorie shared with Norton her feelings about the hard times at the Creek. She also told him about her joy when things went well. Eight years after her divorce from Charles, Marjorie and Norton were married. Norton had to spend time at his hotel in St. Augustine, and she spent time there too. She also had a cottage at nearby Crescent Beach. However, Marjorie still spent much of her time at Cross Creek. It

Norton Baskin, Marjorie's second husband (From Marjorie Kinnan Rawlings Collection, Department of Special and Area Studies Collections, George A. Smathers Libraries, University of Florida)

was an important part of her inspiration to write.

More of Marjorie's work was published. *When the Whippoorwill* was a collection of her short stories. It included "Benny and the Bird Dogs" and "A Crop of Beans." People now wanted to read all of her stories, and everything seemed to be going well. In 1942, just a year after her marriage to Norton, *Cross Creek* was published. That book would change their lives.

Up to that time, Marjorie had written *stories* about the Crackers. She knew her neighbors, the animals, and the plants so well. In *Cross Creek*, her descriptions of the place were, as always, very accurate. Marjorie worked hard at getting just the right words to describe a magnolia tree. One of her readers said she could almost smell the sweet perfume of the blossoms!

But *Cross Creek* was a chronicle. This means it was an honest telling about things that had happened during the fourteen years she had lived there. It was also honest about the people she had met. Her friends had given her much information because they trusted her. So in *Cross Creek*, Marjorie described real people and real events, and used real names.

She invited her readers into her world by describing Cross Creek exactly as she knew it. Since she admired and appreciated her neighbors, she described many of them. She hoped her readers would appreciate them as well. She and Max Perkins talked about whether to use real names. Maybe someone might not like what she said about them. They thought about changing them to made-up names.

Finally, she made her choice. Marjorie decided the story would be the truth about what she experienced at the Creek. For her that meant using the real names.

Marjorie thought she had that right as an author. She thought her neighbors, who were her friends, wouldn't mind. *Cross Creek* was published, and again, people in many parts of the world read and loved the book. It was a huge success. Marjorie received many letters from her readers, thanking her for sharing her thoughts about these real people she had come to love and respect at Cross Creek.

Chapter 8

Problems at the Creek

Marjorie's choice about using real names changed her life. Zelma Cason was one of the first people Marjorie had met at the Creek. They had been friends for years. Marjorie was astonished when she learned that Zelma was taking her to court. Zelma said she was unhappy with the way she was described in *Cross Creek.*

The trial began in 1943. Marjorie's lawyers brought in witnesses to say that she had meant no harm. They said that Marjorie had simply described everything and everyone as she had seen them. Other neighbors did not have a problem with the use of their real names. In fact, they showed strong support of this author who had made Cross Creek known around the world. She had always shown respect and love towards them. They returned that respect and love when she needed them.

Marjorie defended herself by explaining how she

had so thoroughly enjoyed living at Cross Creek. She said that "*Cross Creek* is a love story, of my love for the land." She had wanted to share that love with her readers, inviting them to join in her happiness.

The court case went on for about five years. It ended with Marjorie paying only one dollar directly to Zelma Cason. Unfortunately, Marjorie also had to pay the expensive court costs. The experience had exhausted her.

She continued to write, but would not write much more about the Crackers. Although she still loved her home in Cross Creek, she spent more time at her cottage at Crescent Beach or with Norton in St. Augustine. She also bought a house in New York State. She called it her Yankee house. She did some of the writing on her next book there.

For ten long, hard years she worked on *The Sojourner*, the story of a Michigan farmer shortly after the Civil War. In this book, she was remembering the way of life at her grandparents' farm in that Northern state. But writing had become *very* hard work, and she was tired.

Then she learned that her trusted friend and editor, Maxwell Perkins, had died. Marjorie wondered if she could go on writing without Max's help and support. At last she was able to set aside her grief. She realized that he would have wanted her to keep on telling her stories.

The Sojourner, published in 1953, was never as popular as her Cracker stories. Her writing was interesting, but her readers did not feel the excitement of her earlier books.

Illnesses through the years, the strain of the court case, and the pressure of finishing her last book were just too much for Marjorie. She was at Crescent Beach when she became seriously ill. She died on December 14, 1953, at the age of 57.

Marjorie Kinnan Rawlings was buried not far from her beloved Cross Creek. She was laid to rest at Antioch Cemetery, near Island Grove. Norton Baskin, her husband, wrote the words that were inscribed on her tombstone: "Through her writings she endeared herself to the people of the world."

Marjorie Kinnan Rawlings, 1953. *(Courtesy of the State Archives of Florida)*

Chapter 9

Remembering

Marjorie Kinnan Rawlings' works were read by many people all around the world. In fact, many of her books and stories are still in print, and selling well, today. *The Yearling* and *Cross Creek* are considered to be classics because of Marjorie's style of writing.

Marjorie knew that there are two kinds of writers. There is the one who writes just because it's a job. And there is the one who writes because of the passion to write. If a person has a story inside that needs to be written down and shared with others, that person can write no matter what. A real writer will write even if he or she is not sure the writing will ever be published. The person just *has* to write. As Marjorie said: "He writes because he must. It is his life."

When Marjorie first came to central Florida, she felt a great excitement about Cross Creek and the people living there. That excitement never left her. She translated her feelings into words, even though it was very hard sometimes. She wanted to allow her readers into that marvelous world by using exactly the right words. Luckily, she had the support of her dear friend and editor, Max Perkins, along with many other friends. With their help, she created works that will inspire her readers and other writers for years to come.

As often as she could, Rawlings reached out to other writers to tell them that they too could express themselves in writing. They just needed to be determined to work at their stories. They had to write about something that really, truly excited them.

Marjorie's home and orange grove were donated to the University of Florida in Gainesville. Her precious papers filled with notes about people and places in and around Cross Creek were also given to the university. The papers are kept safe as part of the Special Collections at the University Library. Her very special home in the Florida woods is now the Marjorie Kinnan Rawlings Historic State Park. You can visit there and see where she lived and wrote.

There have been some changes since "Miz Rawlins" lived there. But if you pay attention as you visit the park, you can still see why Marjorie loved the place so much. What used to be an old, rutted dirt road going by her house has now been paved. This makes it easier for the many visitors to get to Cross Creek. They come by the thousands each year from many states and countries.

But the palm table is still on the front porch. Baby ducks, chickens, and a cat still wander through the yard. And who knows—maybe a black snake still uses the path that Marjorie watched. From time to time, park rangers will even give the many visitors another remembrance of the famous author—some fresh orange jam and hot cornbread from Marjorie's recipes.

The Cross Creek of Marjorie's day will never be far from us. She was such an excellent writer that her home and the Cracker families living in those backwoods will always live in her many books and stories. An author's words on a page can sometimes take us to other worlds. The words chosen so carefully by Marjorie Kinnan Rawlings will live on in our memories and enrich our lives for a long time to come.

Afterword

Marjorie Kinnan Rawlings Baskin lived a full, rich life. She was a city girl who found her place of inspiration in the Florida backwoods. She became famous and traveled to many parts of the world. But she always came back home to Cross Creek.

Her writing ability was a rare gift, combined with a lot of hard work. She struggled to put words on paper that would have her readers truly understand the Cracker way of life. She wanted them to almost taste and smell what she described. Her readers laughed and cried because of her words. She was open to all life had for her. She loved the quietness of Cross Creek. She also loved company and made friends easily. She treated people with respect, whether it was the wife of a president or a neighbor in the backwoods. Even after the Cross Creek trial, she remained close friends with many of the people living at the Creek. She was there for them when they needed help, and they were there for her.

Marjorie Kinnan Rawlings paid attention to every word she wrote. And now, years later, in our imaginations we can still be with this author at Cross Creek, the place she loved so much. The reddy-birds and the antses, Jody Baxter, Flag the deer, and her many other characters will remain a part of Florida's history. Marjorie Kinnan Rawlings brought them to life, and they will live on in her wonderful stories.

To See and Do

Marjorie Kinnan Rawlings Historic State Park

18700 S. CR 325
Cross Creek, FL 32640
www.floridastateparks.org/marjoriekinnanrawlings/
Phone: 352-466-3672 (Call for reservations for guided tours.)

While you're there, you might want to ask how Aunt Martha Mickens made fresh butter from milk from Dora the cow.

Glossary

accurately – correctly

brittle – hard, can break easily

editor – a person who gets material ready for publishing

enrich – to add greater value, to make richer

exclaim – to cry out or speak suddenly

grove – a small stand of fruit-bearing trees, especially citrus

horizon – the line between earth and sky

major – a student's special field of study

novel – a book-length, made-up story

sojourner – a visitor, a person who stays for a short time

tenant house – a house where workers might stay

typewriter – a machine that prints letters and numbers by pressing on the keys

turpentine – a liquid coming from pine trees, sometimes used in painting

whippoorwill – a North American bird that repeats a song that sounds like "whip-poor-will"

Yankee – a person who lives in the Northeast U.S.

Selected Bibliography

Bigelow, Gordon. *Frontier Eden: The Literary Career of Marjorie Kinnan Rawlings*. Gainesville, Florida: University of Florida Press, 1966.

Bigham, Julia Scribner, ed. *The Marjorie Rawlings Reader*. New York: Charles Scribner's Sons, 1956.

Rawlings, Marjorie Kinnan. *Cross Creek*. New York: Collier Books, Macmillan Publishing Company, 1987.

Rawlings, Marjorie Kinnan. *The Yearling*. New York: Charles Scribner's Sons, 1966.

Silverthorne, Elizabeth. *Marjorie Kinnan Rawlings: Sojourner at Cross Creek*. Woodstock, NY: The Overlook Press, 1988.

Tarr, Rodger L., ed. *Max and Marjorie: The Correspondence between Maxwell E. Perkins and Marjorie Kinnan Rawlings*. Gainesville, Florida: University Press of Florida, 1999.

References

Note: "Ibid." is short for the Latin word *ibidem*, which means "in the same place." Below, if you see "ibid.," that means a quote came from the same book as the quote before it did.

Dedication page

"Look deep into nature...": Albert Einstein, quoted at www.quotegarden.com/nature.html.

Chapter 1

Page 4. "Peaches.": From page 13 of *Marjorie Kinnan Rawlings: Sojourner at Cross Creek,* © 1988 by Elizabeth Silverthorne. Published by The Overlook Press, New York, New York.

Page 4. "...the joy of my life...": Ibid., 13.

Page 7. "Let's sell everything…": Gordon Bigelow, *Frontier Eden: The Literary Career of Marjorie Kinnan Rawlings* (Gainesville, Florida: University of Florida Press, 1966), 3.

Chapter 5

Page 15. "vibrating with material like a hive of bees in swarm": Ibid., 13.

Chapter 6

Page 18. "I'll tell you what *The Yearling* has done for me…": Rodger L. Tarr, *Max and Marjorie: The Correspondence Between Maxwell E. Perkins and Marjorie Kinnan Rawlings* (Gainesville, Florida: University of Florida Press, 1999), 324.

Chapter 8

Page 22. "*Cross Creek* is a love story…": Gordon Bigelow, *Frontier Eden: The Literary Career of Marjorie Kinnan Rawlings* (Gainesville, Florida: University of Florida Press, 1966), 43.

Page 23. "Through her writings…": From page 349 of *Marjorie Kinnan Rawlings: Sojourner at Cross Creek,* © 1988 by Elizabeth Silverthorne. Published by The Overlook Press, New York, New York.

Chapter 9

Page 24. "He writes because he must…": Ibid., 292.

Acknowledgments

Many thanks to Sheila Barnes, Park Ranger with the Florida Park Service, who has worked at the Marjorie Kinnan Rawlings Historic State Park for the past fifteen years; Florence Turcotte, Curator of the Marjorie Kinnan Rawlings Collection at the Smathers Library, University of Florida at Gainesville; and Phyllis Hansen, Trustee of the Marjorie Kinnan Rawlings Society.

In Charlotte County Public Schools: Thanks to Donna Dunakey, Curriculum and Instruction Specialist, Social Sciences PreK–12; Sandra Rink, Fourth Grade Teacher, Deep Creek Elementary; Nancy Ehrnsberger, Fourth Grade Teacher, Liberty Elementary. In Sarasota County Public Schools: Ms. Lois Collins, Fourth Grade Teacher, Englewood Elementary; and students Zia Kopolovic and Marissa Bentz.

To Cora Bush, friend from Nova Scotia and visitor to Florida, who read over my manuscript and immediately wanted to read Ms. Rawlings' *Cross Creek*; Hallie Schiffman, good neighbor and a very bright third grader; and Bob Sammons.

Thanks to Nina McGuire, a very dear friend and publisher of the first edition of this work, and David and June Cussen of Pineapple Press, who realized the need for a new edition. Thanks as well to Heather Waters at Pineapple Press for her editorial assistance.

And finally, thanks to the many librarians, especially at the Elsie Quirk Library in Englewood, Florida, who have been so helpful with many inter-library loan materials.

Index

About the Author

Sandra Wallus Sammons moved from Pennsylvania to Florida and became fascinated with the Sunshine State's history. As an elementary school librarian in Lake County, Florida, she learned of the need for books on Florida's history on a fourth-grade reading level. She began writing biographies of fascinating Floridians. So many lived such inspirational lives. She now lives in central Florida with her husband and their black cat, Spades.